T0114901

MAN
FROM
MARCH

TIMOTHY GREEN

author HOUSE

AuthorHouse™ UK
1663 Liberty Drive
Bloomington, IN 47403 USA
www.authorhouse.co.uk
Phone: UK TFN: 0800 0148641 (Toll Free inside the UK)
*   UK Local: (02) 0369 56322 (+44 20 3695 6322 from outside the UK)*

© 2023 Timothy Green. All rights reserved.

No part of this book may be reproduced, stored in a retrieval system, or transmitted by any means without the written permission of the author.

Published by AuthorHouse 07/14/2023

ISBN: 979-8-8230-8267-9 (sc)
ISBN: 979-8-8230-8273-0 (e)

Print information available on the last page.

Any people depicted in stock imagery provided by Getty Images are models, and such images are being used for illustrative purposes only.
Certain stock imagery © Getty Images.

This book is printed on acid-free paper.

Because of the dynamic nature of the Internet, any web addresses or links contained in this book may have changed since publication and may no longer be valid. The views expressed in this work are solely those of the author and do not necessarily reflect the views of the publisher, and the publisher hereby disclaims any responsibility for them.

beneath

The undercarriage of the royal carriage
carrying a constellation of broken men
that broke way before battle
beneath the wholesome futile of reality.
Powers that be would have early
Muscling in on a a phrase with high tone
my body is my fathers, not my own
crowning him with a glorious win
times come together, bring me in
Journeying from A to Z
i missed a letter a a number
she said she would wait
well i am still waiting
for the plaiting of my greying hair.
depicting from a element of power
because the stay is not mine
wetting in mud and dirt, grease and grime
without moaning and complaining
because they are serving with hope in their eyes
reprise of hope and changes lead home
because i carry my wait
debating to bring a sense of years
bring on my way, praying to cease
the wars and torments
of this deceased land.
beneath the way the world works
undercover

1

The forgotten child

My tendons, my bones, my joints
yielded to the point of heavy brazen points
Secure in its own way
My key-dog is a its way to the throne
where i come boldly and confidently
because i am saved, my daddy says so
    But in this echo, sense no meaning
believed but out of touch with reality
what is reality when it bites?
jolted into multiplied of heights
politely given a beginning heart
the forgotten child rises a clouds
in victory.
    Mountains hinder my walk
but my battle scar, has no objection
to my high flying protection
Prickles is real to the point of death
colors and sentiments uncaught my spirit
when it comes and goes, twists and throws
Call me a saint, call me a brother
because that is who i am
no other love but my own
disowned by the world but not by my own
The forgotten child, forgotten rivers and valleys
my ways are your ways LORD, in the sunshine

Sent

The present you favour
because i am your heavenly neighbour.
the sorrow of those whom believe
Writ me into history
where space and time is a mystery
thrifting and sifting
Polite delights that light the night
because you are the one that aids
because you love is all that is said
Misword letters and unfettered chain mail.
Sailing across the tossing wind
find me the code that has your print
feeling your words and unbounded lines
that deliver our generation for ylatctre
New sentence and a new prologue
beating the odds and fears that fall
fall on your orders and happy your children
I was sent to defend your cause
I am sent to free her lands I cuse
Dancing slightly a yolate sandware comes
rushing over me, front and back

3

recieve

i retrieve my hopes and fears
even after all of these years.
courage sees me years through the waters
stay as they maybe
My lived stories of life and love
Strange, its ways that bend a tender feeling
breaking the bread that feeds and gives life
I counter-act those belligerent days
where it was one for me and one for the other
Pass me my shield
kindly i say to the sea farers.
cast out and bring in the catch.
it will feed you for life.
because with you i sleep at night.
I live in the city, how wanna am I?
it is the way of the world
it is the way i take in my catch
I rely on you and your blessings
resting in the brick enforced dwelling
that carried me through childhood.
receive and i shall bless you, massively

4

Following

Wherever you want me to go
i shall follow you round
Wherever you want me to feel
I feel in your thoughts.
Wherever you need to talk
I shall be your aid
Wherever you want to look upon me
You have the lense to see.

However you say i love you
however soft or cracked
the voice that comes from the void
Even if it had been touched
I come back to the art of the heart
Parting waves, parting ways
Not try to discredit you
but whatever the weather, you shine
I don't mind about the colour
I don't care about such weather
but i care about you
This is what i say about it
Every gaze and day brings something new

Equality

Do you know that we are equals?
Another yet of that sequel
Setting you down and crowning you glory
all i have to say is that i adore thee
Poor to me the money; all saw
the buried board can testify.
I am innocent in equality with you
Kind and elegant my sentinel awaits
My cave is barren, now i go home.
to a place where possibilities roam
Opportunity carries you good
You good fellows troupe
The passage that i threw is safe
Made in a bit youth.
And you are following in my tracks
It matters that you are coming back
brave warrior and strong visitor
You are i can want a
frozen in time, preserved, adored
You woke up and declare
My LORD, are you there? Yes.

Passing through the elements.

Wishing for you every joy
I employ you every success
Stature that follows my voice
Passing through the elements
Sentiments amount my goals
Should at the happy seas
Easily brought my sense
Save all yourself, my purpose
Chasing the waters land
the parts that keep me grounded
Sanctify my voice
its my choice i do this
for you, and with you.

have what they say about time
times not elements they me attract
time is no commodity.
We must take our chances
and stand by our voices
elements yes and so does time
but what is the other side of then.
elements end, that is it. Time ends
then there is a new start

Cast me your cares

because of your glistening star
i want you in and out
basking with the constant arrays
it is my day that i shall sing
prevailed to customary change
the age of curtains calling
enthralled by a lasting wave
Wishing i could reach that way
behaving in a way that brings
Swings and ropes
Stroking and taking
but before i go i shall show
your life has a calling.

5/3/2023   Timothy Crea

two thirds behind
the days of my mind
Reveal if you count me fit?
i desire your kiss
there are few things more,
that is desire to me
fluffing my wives in all sorts.
as i cast my mind back
Centuries of color set me aback
there are no other allowances
that i prepare to gauge.
A new start, a new page
is it really just my age?
but i have a lot to give

5/7/2025   Tin Wren

Powers that be

I call to you
out of the thin air
Preparing to survive
stare at me if you dare
hairs of the hair stand up.
I sing with you through glass
Calling me back from the brink
Sinking into your seat
breath with me, in me
My stirring nature builds me up
About my age yr hedge cars
Start me up, the single way
thru and throw, set it away

10

Prozac

Feeling in a relaxed mood,
tuned into my own Station.
what a hungry brood
Not, which rail stopped watching
reversing a feeling of awesome plunder
seems all oh so real
With zest and journeys riddle
best of rest on,
where i realise my supply
   Prozac is the cure of my sadness
Senseless and emotionless
but i am still here
My life has changed so dramatically
No longer a fanatic drunk
and i realise my real supply
the one that keeps me fed and nurtured
further so ban the truth
i could go further, but i don't have to
Subdued in its own sense
my heart belongs to me
and that is what i am saying.

11

40 Shades of Green.

Colours that bone me
Green of every state
Plating my green mossy fruits
Notices of a acute injury
taking years to heal
My heart it really does feel at home now
A blow to the head causes damage
A blow to the heart causes death
Manage the ways we feel
Past ways could be the way
that leaves us to gateway
the reside of passion and elements.
all gone astray
40 shades of Green in the forrest
20 Shades of Grey in the city
10 Shades of blue in the sky
1 Shade of water, one that matches my tears
4 carry years of regret.
A true behind every rejection —
Is equalled with every collateral
Possession is 9/10ths of.

12

Chumming up.

You get yourself out of bed
there is further use for you yet.
Do not regret the leaving of the sky
Sunset, sunrise, it is all in you eyes
If you despise the good you have
What shall become of the bad?
Talking with you i do declare
i wish not to talk, no single word
So i shall leave soon.
and go to somewhere far, far away.

i find you again

because you are who you are
Taking my place beyond the star
for because i wanted you close
i touch the most high
Surprising the very solid rocks
Dropping by the doctors.
because if you rage and rage.
what do other people say?
Raging over the sea
Can we reasonably direct power
because you are just and true
i find the pressure is on me
but you take it all away.
Chasing rainbows and blowing gales.
failing to admit defeat.
This rock spurts out water
and everything that sustains.
Voyages that range far a distance
Drought online for disaster
Many journeys of shitty duties
Sending you again, the lonely anger

Penance for a pittance

When i see your youthful stories
you store them up for me.
When i ask of your deliverance
it is always beside thee
When i believed in eternal
and the pain felt unending
When i search your mind
i feel a inner pull on my heart
The pull of a weighty ambition
to be who you already are
and then i see within myself
that you bring me your healthy wealth
No prodding a pulling a nursing
but the matter of truth is
is that you are discovery
furthering the Kingdom in weight
Weighty, Godly ambition floods
right to the survival and service
of my natural children
children of faith and yours
A child just like you

felt my worth today

Worthy are the children of God
My Father counts me a blessing
and when i jest lightly
Oh, how high we really do fly
and fly is what we did
at one with my kite
Delicately flickering here and there
Ducking and diving, i found you near
Today i separate myself from this things
Evil plots that strikes of rotten Sorrow
Tomorrow they may have
but what of yesterday?
A place that fills me with wonder
or places that have no walls
a ceiling or floors.
The tides flow in and rattle the ground
Run aground or those with no place.
This place that you run with
i believe is your empathetic mission
to bring others hope and joy
you have a eternal purpose my boy

Inside the mind.

Oh be so kind to lend me your pen?
because i get so cold without it
You speak to me through your words
and i feel un-deserving
did i miss-hear your weighty praise?
because weighty they are.
Struck i am by your smile
it is worth while trying for.
hitting the floor with you did
harmed my senses and erotical state
You feel like it is in you
to do the best i can do
and i am flattered by your persistence
because we need ya, minds like yours
and i have figured something out
that you know me and what i am worth
there is no price to pay, it has been paid.
So i snuggle up in your kind mind
laying beside, know you are safe
in the knowledge that you are
a yet i am not my glass and goods

17

Burning Pebbles

These intricate moments we cherish
Replenishing your spirit
and everything is and with it
They bounce, these ideas
ideas dissapearing like jelly
Pebbles i bounce off my water
Skip they do until they finish their journey
come in and tell me, show me
that all is well
Excelling in a body of praise and joy
You make us fearful my ...
So be still, and know that i am God
Your Father and healer, protector and free-spirit
free as the birds of the air
tell me your wants and needs
because i can make you great
i want you to see the promise land
the music is yours
but Remember that you are my member
Don't be shy, you are precious to me
be fair, be wise, be strong, be safe.
xxx

18

Filled of my voice.

You fill me with my choice
to keep you and share my voice
filling me with my chance to shine
and surely I do carry you
believing you can shine to not a fault
all I see is you start of the heart
My sound I leave with you
it shall reach the multitude
and your good fruit shall blossom and grow
because I connected you to my people
we are brothers and I honour you
find me a place amongst your people
Yearning it is hard to break free
from these ideas and ideals
free holding me back.
You are the light of my world
how could I ever comprise?
but I hear you and you kindly
as the figures that dance across your sky
Wisely I love to say
Lord, have I your way in me!

Trembling

I see you, your status, your majesty
are i for you at times?
behind the hits and scenes
I blame my cure and the worry begins
My inhibition and my ...
following you as the weather takes me
into those ... to be filled
angst and anxiety takes me brightly a ...
... your summer heat that parades this way
Directness, i act politely
Detaches, i mean ... fashion
Rejections are not in my cabinet
I see you fit to finish the race for my canyon
Stumbling and humbling, i hid my way
the pressure was off for the day
headborn and not led to reason
I channel you a ...
be bold, be big, be much inside
but let no one know that you ... gripping ...
this world and its separation
... and folding, my just occasion

holding on

I sense an unanswered trepidation
the colors you see a separation
Nations rise up against each other
What am i to do about it?
Casting your cares on this world
would deny them their power
rights to reign or fall
is it a wonder i see it all?
Saw this their eyes and, i see the mother
nursing a broken child
that has senselessly been beaten
My heart is with them and i sense a way
they carry on with them each day we pray
Don't abandon your calling of priesthood
Changing they try to release you
but you are my friend and i deliver you
because you shook and screamed on your bed
So you came to rising on the tide
the tide is out, now what about that that will?
increased by fear, clearly i resign.
From earthly work and a ride of chaste.

21

Faces

Defacing the very nature of hope
It is a travesty that legs waste the garden
Pardoned and matured my feelings killer
Drilled in color and shine
I leave my heart in your hands
Planned in haste to renew the face
But then again you taste you freedom
My martyr and challenger
of the world's ways
    unfazed by you waves that smash the earth
faces that come by and unremembered
thus remembered as the body is dis-muttered
hopes and dreams of the seams of the coast
where mostly i wrongly behave
Save me Lord because i share
Earth's issues and problems.
i try to solve them through prayer
No soothsayer have a say
because this is the way i prayed
heavenly hosts come for us.
Our protection is in their hands

22

I found you

My collection retracts its shape and form
but before i give my heart to you
first i must be sure we will ring it true
Shapely deliverance comes for my few
chewing and brewing my plan of escape
Makes me melt such as the heartache.
because deliverance comes in many forms
Is it normal to want you so much more?
Creeping and tracking where you go.
I finally found my love waiting in the snow.
Declaring the truth to sow the seeds
Feeding my lambs, oh what a treat
because you are kind to my people
I shall honor you
because you give so readily to yourself.
I shall send an elevator, right up to me.
Choices, you make the right ones
A studious soul that will be unearthed
You honor me with your smile and words
Creatively adept and worries, know, sleep.
Dripped and shripped, you breath gold
In your costing i feel the right part.

Courting the poet.

I plotted my very casting ways
Praise in my name, taming reason.
Families wait to address my words
With you reason is lost in the heart
heard the very prominence of you gone
Soldering in into each other.
Creating creativity that flows and collects.
how did i find myself here?
because you sad tears i struggle to bare
I learn nothing, no-one and even the chair support
if an object can support as they do.
Think of the possibilities between me and you.
the dreamscape cares many a soul
due to the militia, i know my work.
Daring to care me in and out of the earth
birthed and deserving of a righteous halo.
Born to care and disarm the soldier
Smouldering is my love that cares the air.
Staring intently into ares eyes
lasting and grasping re-current supplies
live for me, i sched you heart, declare me
very inward poet.

My text message.

They beep wakes me up from my sleep.
Ringing in my delicate ear
Fearing a looming heavy sensation
this nation need me awake
Don't forschu it but remche it.
frosty movements sent into a penance.
My wanton message from my love.
another Kid charms the senses.
Fermenting the raging box full of a yes
I switch it off and make off my stakes
blocking the building box that holds me strong
We belong to every pure and single things.
It is because I bring my loved prince
away from the supplimating sentrialed society.
Society that led me away from home.
Cause whatever yet of my own
I refuse and take the mail.
But it a strange way to say i feel
kneeling down at my sorcerers feet
Planting a kiss meekly seeking deliverance
the yardline is to much to bear
by your side. you will find me there

25

because you are here.

So dear to me you are my face
when i see you in the mirror
you get better looking each day.
playing my way around the fray.
Connected in a strange and unusual way
i was thinking of you yesterday.
when i cast adrift my ties and pray.
because you come to me, you are so dear
clearing my way and my throat
It's your protective spirit, just like a moat
Cloaked in heaven respite is here
fear has no collateral over me
Palm beaches in my mindful state
It's the color you place me in.
I have yet further plans.
And try to lay them gently on you.
Counting the days when i will see you too
Erasing sad tonal elements
Pretense and resentment gone
Plodding into the strong arms of my love
Cloaked in quiet and unusually good state
                                        of mind.

This fading pain in my head.

Running to you, i find my home
Running this race i lead ad room
it is the place i call my own.
focusing at the mark of maintaining pressure
Measured in my lively weighty proof.
that i am not all there
Prepare me for the future
When i need my LORD to fight for me.
I am prepared to take all of the heavy weight
But i need your presence
to freight me to somewhere no-one knows
No-one but you
I tend to chew my words with a you mark
heading south i rough-it for a while.
but when did i ever have to rough-it?
That cumbersome pain in the head is fading
Making a cutsize of thoughts brought towards
into my temporary state of mind.
Temporary because the pain fades into nothing

27

Counting the sparrow

because of the seam
That seems to be splitting
My ink cracks, what of the setting?
betting that for miles
I can see the heavens age
all the earth shall know your name
even the sparrow and its frame
Its like a counting of souls
Sparrows last for a little while
but leaves a lasting impression.
I smile as i see them grow
bigger and higher, row by row.
Set amongst the trees
On its knees it waits
for the gates to open
and rises above the earth
It deserves to be so
and fixed in what i will do
Sow the seed and begin to breathe
Sometimes it is so hard to see
what is beneath

The test

The change of chambermaids
At the door a complete change.
As the tables are, i don't remember names
Watches for names, what a stupid way
i wish to detect how this strange world
Curling underneath a willow tree
I have found myself waiting and waiting
Would storms happen, but not a us.
Testing constantly whatever or wherever
is the miss-trust i have grown to know
the testamental qualities
That do seem to be a novelty
in this current past and future
Modelling my clothes to see if they fit.
I have disarmed a robot
And now is the test to see if we are legit
fluttering and tottering a the bird
Older and now wise
I call myself a climber
Resultant changes and weigh managing my void
until tomorrow, and then we shall voice again.

Newness inside you

Carousing plausible feelings
that strobe through smoke inhaled objectivities.
Mention me and all of my protesties.
Projected onto the ceiling, even the sky
I ask for more but i do not know why.
Surprise me sometime
Your sublime sensory perception meets
full of a world of rejection
Taking your stance against ill-fated dream
Newness inside you dragging the feet
of a individual is unique proportion.
Those feet, comfortable in time
winding and letting go.
What's the use to brix what is lucky?
Underneath and above me
the stars sense a strain.
but i am bubbling over with serenity
if you can? is it possible
to inflict such pain, taking the strain
and then letting it all go, the control
is there because if it wasn't, where would
                                        we be?

30

thinking of you

Calmly he touches the paper
with lips so sure as a neighbor
My savior, my neighbor
enabling my freedom to be reality.
Majestic in this ways.
Seeing a marmel on the pavement
jumping to his aid
Surrounded villages
and understanding the yoke.
I shall talk and not be silent
the world may grow so
but i have disrupted my bo
Sure to release a blessed word
I am unarmed but not unprepared
imprisonments seem my catch
the one that breaks. the final fortune
of fortune so wild you walk and strive to
turn a corner, dive for cover
as there are people who kill for it.
Thinking of you and you humble reigns
I am here and shall always be

31

brilliance, all in white

Past collection and collection.
raise a quest and to possibilities
i send my core in the stare of my modern
don't forsake you neighbour
as i sense my modern service.
cable ties and whips and bullet
cannot stop gods glow, full or not.
excusing into a sky report filled room
judged by others, but not with tomb-ward
its a possible notion to drink the death yolk
and not die.
brilliance, all in white.
the corpse service survives me
trickling my purpose related blood
found a pile of mis-understood bodies
they can be bold on my embodiment raise
the alarm that leads my taste
hastily i bring to you my glean
LORD, please remember me as you fried a servant.
riding up in my pure white horse
because you are the survive
of the modern day news.
cheering and spitting at the floor
the distaste make you sick
costing at the brick built prison

brassy ensemble.

Bands of brothers call in time
further still a sense of wine
towards the hill i sense their gaze
its over to you LORD, we have the title
Chiding you the nurturing place
Times and dates all erased
Picking up my wholesome meal
currently sealed in my bosom
Critic comes and harvests are made
bring to us the LORD and his frame
Maids sent to look after us needs
breath in me Still
as i am up to my knees in silt
Mud being my armor
i rise without note a cause to charm
Palms dry, i sense why
because his faith is strong
brassy britches, twitching from fear
my servant and teacher, what a need
Unique in essence, needed indeed
relax my bones and back into my steed.

33

Cooking up something

boldly and coldly re-feathered
dress me up as I am tenderly waiting
was naked and prepared to be consumed
then my maker, creator, father and hero
took me away from death and destruction.
Stories came apart with no morals or direction
Subtle defence and defiance of the odds
the rod would have beaten me if it could
seems the law was broken, soaked in blood
strodious, waiting, generating speed to face
face-offs, the line has been set, planted
scathing reports that distort the truth.
Youthful expression suddenly dis-proved.
You soothe my candid soul into a substance
that is reluctant to halt my journeys path.
endorse my time and methods of her flight.
because it takes time to remember greatness
parades set in-crimson red, turning heads to wonder
You are cooking up something i have never tasted
like the wind captured in bottles, put to the tip.
Gripped by sipping a thousand of your best thoughts.
My meal i didn't have to shoot, as they are shorts.
grass fit for the birds, oatmeal for the herds
but it is us whom carry tomorrow
another plate, another show

34

My new curfew   13/2/23

As i stand among the rebels and that authority
charged any attempted my nameless shame
because of you i carry the tide
along the weedy, green crazy curfews
I do not mince my words
Casting my curses and blessings
those nesting birds catch a glimpse of them
because yours is mine, and i carry it downwind
Elements really do stage monumental efforts
to encage the hosts in the shivering clouds
they hug and linger then crash awkwardly,
hanging onto your every word
because you bring plenantries un named
to the tender, heaven bound voices.
Pressed into the bosom of the lightest flower.
Can i reside in you, so i know you are true
brewing my sweet, perfectly made soul
it comes into my arms so i lay down my throne
Knowing all to well that if i wait but.
Casting you to be the deliverer of good news
take a pew with the revered few
Praise and honor belongs to the father
i cannot boast, it belongs to him
                    Tim G.

Sunday

How i wish to be yet of you
Melancholy silences brush past me
Since i became someone new
Past effects and realities ring true
Sunday coming up
Lots to see and think about
bringing the pain without a cloud.
Surrounded by coloured visuals
It's no wonder how i came to be
Planned souls searched and found
Pounding in the chest of a door
badgering a genius
Insanity of enemies drawn to brush
but what i sense most
it is your day and she is the host.
You may have little, but you have a lot.
I am here to disprove a myth
to ruin it.
belonging to me has its merits
favour, food and in most pleasing thoughts
Tumbling into a world of love.

36

board Walk

before you finished your sentence
a chill came over me as i stood
to deliver the goods
i caved to your suggestion
of netting a potential profit
what profits a man
to loose himself to gain recognition?
    Then you turned to me and asked,
what is this test you have given me?
why do i learn so slow, yet grow so fast?
the board walk is calling,
years of brutality and fear vanquished.
in a distant moment around me
i sense a realistic turn of events
presenting itself to me at my aid
paid for a job done at the finish
hunger and devoid of comfort
i rehearse the lines i want to say
but i know it will be another way
as we pray for a beginning
and an end of the boardwalk

37

Riots in the bars

is it your divine right to riot in bars?
can i trust you chick and say it is ours?
because i languorously remember a time
that you could speak to a neighbor
...the elements of world topics
no longer talk of religion or faith
Politics raises it brazen head
to disperse what once was held sacred
teaching the real sympathy the maimed man
married to the point of unrecognition
but be we the beggars
revellers in the sight of man
Nowadays you hear blacks treated silly
but life takers and baby killers
live a lofty height we die jorged on
prison and detention for doing right?
Sad state of the world we are in
we begin to shake until it changes
the world will not age into submission
but the church is expected to adhere
to the mood and rules of the land
kept in fear, the plan is to take back
what once was ours for the keeping
riots in the bars, we wall read to go far
to find you loud.

for ya policy

Honestly i say to ya heart
Start as ya mean to go on
I shall not depart from you
what a see ya soon
With a song in ca hearts.
Carry my weight, contemplate
the state of modern day society
In the middle of night
a all to often by day
Notions of peace pushed aside
Politely i say is it ya pride?
Co-inside with me and my dwelling
Suffer not my poor spelling
Smelling ya historical swelling
as i heed my own content
an i ca policys news?
Releasing the noose of years of abuse
Carry me here, spread me apart
Awash with new color and experience
in my gentleness i cause a stirr
for ya policy, it is a dettriment

39

found

found at sea
i am whom i was meant to be
a total chancer am i
where i see beaty everywhere
hidden treasures
measureless and left alone
your tonal wanderous expression
pressureless, pressured for less
i humbly accept your request
for foreighn aid
portrooyal and its subtlety
raises its own question
      Why?
why am i ablest to run?
all i know is this
      that bliss is now a fantasy
i look to you for my own reality
      stand by
as i wait in the wings for you
i call your name, france becons
weapons forged shall not prosper
waist deep in order the border
caught in action and fractions
inaction is a weapon of destruction
disfuntion clouds my ears

Coming of age

i say you brood the mood
covered with bruises
  but i soothe them
hampered and down in the mouth
Searching north, bearing south
because you are who you are
brittle and unopened
sentimentally emotionally broken
it is a token of my being
brought before the page
as i sense in you a polisher surface
nervous because you are the one
my future is in your hands
knowing you have plans for it
your position, just see me as new
flight carries me through
it is all so near to perfection
ingesting the revelation
this nation needs you father
i would rather it be from you
one of the fewer national treasures
    that pleasure in full measures
feathers tethered by rage
it is time i coloured my page
young at heart, old of age

chasing causes

because my interior changes
i blot along my severred wades
destiny calls across the pages
manage my montage
freely manage the carriage
simply put, i found the way
i pace and erase the trip
you shoot from the hip
take a sip of my sweet sweet water
i do not falter as a missionary
Plotting your journey
flirty and playfully responsive
to your needs, pleasing to touch
knowing such a starring role.
warm to the touch
there can be a lesson learnt
where pain is the name of the game
but we are all the same.
Taming the shrew and the shrewd
moved into suppression
expression realising its mission
ammunition lost in transit
hampering the war deposit
coming out of the closet
needs fulfilled, brilliantly east

When you late

Talking through your cloudy moments
i forget to see your movements
From what i can remember of them.
You are gracefully mine
Urging for your continuity
Communing in a far away place
Generate me into electric fuzz
Pushing you across the floor
I am late once again

but you were early
Living with my state of affairs
i deserve to believe your flair for it
Well explores my chaos
More than whom i am
blowing in the breeze
Counting your deceased past, I forget to add you.
I don't count it against you.
Personally i say with a shrewd look
Another hiding place, another mouth.
Sheath to the legs and wax
Palms breeze and Psalms rise again.

The riverside

We stay in ones, twos, threes and fours
Walking the beach and sandy shores
The food the drink such a treat.
We are heated in the mid-day sunshine.
talking and sharing
talking of blessings
Sentimentally the ships drift in.
As today comes to a close
and the mind comes to rest.
Viewed by the might of someone sea law
not guarded how it end for it.
Sharely i come in peace and givings
Nurturing regardless of mis-givings
bringer of the light he is made of.
Sentimentally fund it you please for us.
blessed we are
leaving enemies to eat dust.
We are trusted with such a commission
My fruity highly regarded pastime
Pausing because i hear your voice
into your beings, my weary heart sure

Am i a slave?

Systematic terrors of the night
Born in blood but forgotten his rights.
You sit politely waiting for the call
Its slavery and the bruises are real
really they belong, but in this song it is real
heading for a exit, an open wound
forced to enable the movement of the moon
The i question myself:
am i a Slave to Society?
or am i just single and vulnerable?
forced to me the guns at will
Yes, it is the military Still
that makes us wait in the wings
but never brought into the spotlight
because that is dangerous for those.
As for me i leave with no regrets
i net a profit and empty my bank
every of the state, whose estate is it?
it is my fathers and all he gives with it
But threaten me, i am not a wastrel
Wandering into my neighbours garden for food

45

Sitting on an idea

It was my idea that i had to think
It was my choice to look to the brink
It was my melody singing into the night
   Meddling with your god given right
to live in a beautiful land
Man the trumpet, keep the horn
I am still here, not a still-born
My medicine is my father
he rallies me up to wake y to gather
the undesirables and prickable run-ins
I was ar meant to protect
but all we do is pretend its ok
when it is not.
Shuttling into a marginal society
Where habits grow into vice and word
Give me a choice over my future
because, am worth murhovins
bring me my gun and sword
drup than at my feet, hroce in a state
Why carry a sword?
When a gun is much lighter?

What delivers?

Waiting and contemplating
on the thrills and spills of creativity.
am i right?, am i wrong?
because this bard sings his song

Delivery yearning and mending bridges
Searching the land for you
Sensing your journey Spurs me on.
Journeys here the habit of changing
rummaging in your mind
becomes that bodily element
fervently yes
It was waiting to be met
completing my ever forming net.
Past regrets gone into oblivion.
Feeling the ground beneath my feet
Completing the delivers my own mystery
Chasing my adventurous side
Calling the birds that made me cry
Crying out to my ever breathing Sentinel
Cementing my place in history
Sisters and brother made strong.

Warmth takes me

When i battle to fill the air
Succumb to my yessing breeze
Peeling a sense of dignity
Getting down on my knees
because you are to be loved and revered
Near to the end one may be
but due to my colours, you adopted me
fortune favours the few
I am fortunate because of you
Useless to end the lightning tyrade
Colours of my own heart
Truly share and glow is yet
to my own dignity and notices it realism.
Whatever is in you, i delight and care in you
blue to the tiles but stars the ache
Grief; i really released my heart of pain.
Sanity returns and i am time again
Maimed but capable of great things
It is my honor to sing this way
Whatever the heart has to offer
offer me a fragrant hello.

East from the west

because you bore me and my voice
i can call you my beloved son
because you chose to do right
our journey of faith has begun
because of my merits i feel much love
all because i was one whom you came for
Saving your life from a lifetime of destruction
Retraction of the world senses the end
of how things are right now
feeling your troubles and you need to air
Pairing off with another secret
Secretly drawn into my honest opinion
Send me someone who can calm the seas
Make me someone who can do wonders
as people think of wonders, weaving not the end
Courageous spirit that caresses my soul
all because you love me so
borrowing your ways that i do not sustain
A world of love, places of your hidden
amongst the dying falling leaves
Separate the sin from me that sometimes
can weigh a me down

49

ice and spice

ice and spice were twins, and they lived in an underground house
they were known as the underpeople. They were very tall people.
in fact they were very short. This was due to the fact
that the tunnels they walked through wrent very high.
ice was the girl twin and she had spark ing green hair with a
cute little turned up nose and purple eyes. She w s quite chubby
in fact, which was quite common for the underpeo ple
Spice, was the boy twin and he had coal black hair and
mischievious blue eyes. Spice was taller than ice, he was
three feet tall and not as chubby as ice. This was due to the
fact that he only ate chocolate i e_ icecream whereas ice only
ate strawberry ice cream because the underpeople as they were

known only had a diet of ice creams , so the fariety was
tremendous and all made with a secret recipe of course
their little houses were made from bricks of ginger biscuits
and the streets were made of marshemallows, the type
that you can walk on. as walking was the only transport
available so no Co2 emissions underground.
                The cows lived in fields a d te apples.
because the milk they produced was very creamy and tasted like
ap ples. So they were beautiful cows but only grew to be two
feet high. They were very smart and friendly.
On this p articular day, ice and spice decided that unthey would
spring clean their house an d replace the bricks made out of
ginger bis cu ts that were crumbling. On tyeir way to the skip
to discuard the brick biscuits they had a plan. The story had
been told to them by the anchients! who were the keepers of the
s tories of the underpeoples history. The reason for this being is
that spice had found a book whilst cleaning their house of their

Parting waves

when i pasted the waves for you
i wanted something resembling praise
Days and nights i heard you cry
for freedom & bondage.
Messengers calmly deliver the mail
it read, "lets keep this amicable"
I would like to see you safe and happy
lets be bold and regweal.
You are investment resting on my shoulders
It may seem like a fixed fitting
but silence in you actual, permitted
Permitting as drug hole to be filled
with what we prefer to eat and ingest
i offer the best ways and home.
but for now i realise it is you ours.
having chosen to buy you hat.
it is something i cannot do
I live in my heat, it is my home.
So wherever i go im filled
You have your way,
and i a ok with that

51

Playfully yours

Kindness often makes its way
away from the rules and problems of today
Playing are our ways to live
Sorted and bought time filled moons
touched they say open to freedom
distilled my own voice
The thought of you brings me round
Providing a yes close
She always use the good spirit
taught my insights to be vigilant
Infinite wisdom from the heart
that seems so far away
We pray and praise the one who can change
all our directions, remedied in an instant
Instantly yours, water so poured
into a response, source and destination.
Always being my attentive attention
Pretend you are who you wait.
Its difficult as counting sheep.
Sleeping in a curved oath
the shore, playfully yours

52

its just a covering

thank you for your timely seclusion and inclusion
 lack of movement insuing discipline removing tenderness
 slightly less implications shown and given to them
  what a massive cover up supping tea through it all
   forgetting the poor and needy seeking comfort
    we seek love and a home, for them collseum and dangers
 the lad is comforted. at home and content
   the law broke the fall and shed us a little skin
skins do vary and ordinarily found   contrary to belief
does belief deny understanding, profound reasoning?
   elements of doubting , flooring the system made to help

   its a sad situation when the hsopitals created to help
   undemine the law that was meant to protect
    surreal as it may seem, dragging hooks for bream
funny how someone lacks capacity after a pitfall
what about the lovers pining for attention getting detained?
 refrained from feeling, believing. filled with hope
 fe athered summits and soft pillows grown from a silver spoon
  the family all send happy returns. returning the call
 to the tall, s mall and un classified tied to a desk
  rantings of the city remaining still to seem just
   mustard gas now turning into bombs and domination
its a repead and we w ant our count y back
   slacken those jaws and s tick around you motionless or bored

the edge

Follow my lead as i lead you a
flowing down the road
My course leads to a geused box
Where treasures and filaments carry
  Purging losses that are tossed
up and down the hill
Not tossed but turned over
the new leaf we pray to
The jaw clicks its last click
As i made a sickly mess
Digesting and ingesting
Caressing broader lois of fire
Desiring to touch the heart
and raise an empire
My Stature erases many an oppression
Successes suppresses the free
As i lead my way to the edge.
Scavaged until you're ad red
Sledging and battling, biting, vicitins
Purposefully years throughout the ages
I turn my year. Like i always do
we be a the save, they have no clue

54

catch me

into your safety
I commend my spirit
nurturing my form
because o my Lord
you care for us

creation ones

sensing its need
to breathe
easily we turn to
you
for
answers
i see issues, you see
solutions, a reason
to be
follow the Joys of life

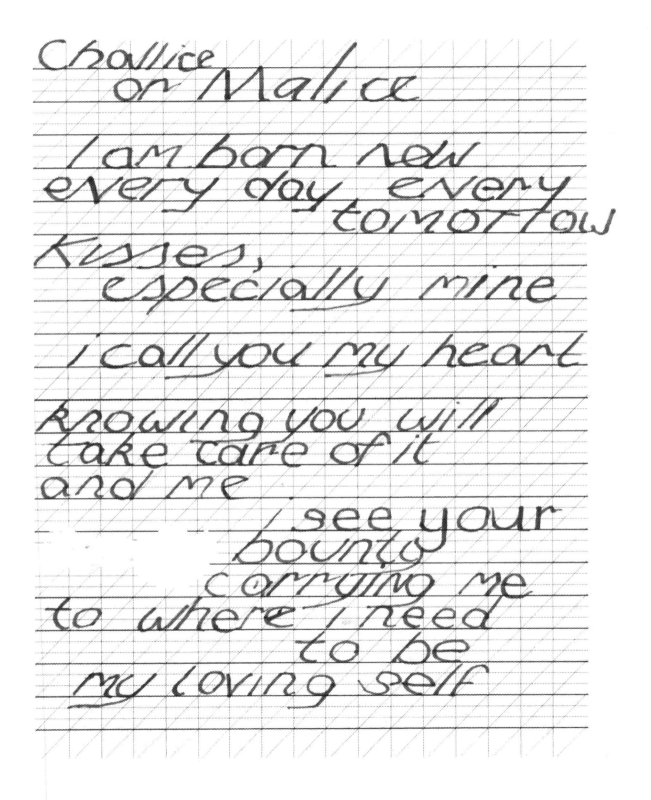

Challice
  or Malice

I am born new
every day every
            tomorrow
kisses,
  especially mine

I call you my heart

knowing you will
take care of it
and me

              see your
              bounty
          carrying me
to where I need
          to be
my loving self

because of you

beauty
        and all its
running elegance
        out
                into the sea
beneth
                those tidal
your   forces
        love be me
for all to see

tranquility finds
                its place
among the
                trivials
of this
        frail world
you
        see my predicament

follow me
distilling my senses
delivering forth my
            allingment
cryingonto
        the
            windy page
nestled into
            my chest
blessed as
i goforth and realise
the dreams i have
with you and for
            you

living among the poor
all that i saw of you was your smile
it blinded me to everything else
kissing it and hoping it will last forever
jumping to its own conclution
where i become my waiting friend
You are waiting for a time you can play
the ticket has been paid for by me
Jump on board and recieve my love
willingly my course is set
homewards, my home is yours
blend and mix to your neighbor
content to fix and transfur the vibe
strong as you be i suggest this:
open yourself up to changing tides
as you ride them, think d me
destination secured
remember me as you fly
rise and sail this world of mine
teach my flock designed by me
completed works, i give you more
youre motives are clear
so sit with me

Sleep while you saw

When you sleep at home
is a safety at you own.
it is a little wonder
you were born to roam

tossing back and forth in the sky
Sleepy little stars, the bright ones
ready to sigh a sigh of relief.
because you are the one
chasing the thief that takes away
and doesn't give back

Sleep while you sow, you are you know
blasting forth rhythm in tow
hugging at the ship's seams
really do give a holla remorse
chasing you till by the bit of any horse
cause us to stir slightly
I must write us politely
and hope you can lead me home
Tinks' gloomy edges revert
to a state of rest
but nevertheless we are bought at a
                    high cost

60

Is it time?

when i feel like i lost it all,
feelings that left me feel so small
answering the call, burst into tears
fears you and, me, belong to you
Call me a stone as i bear with the trouble
of life lost, tears and rubble double
in my head i tend to bend my knee
listmore towards the leave, must be free.
Three times you all dead what about me?
I am truly its you as i follow you
curtesy showing me disowned me
responsibility for creativity
Seeing you reality for punctuality
We pray for a way to going this way.
date and time reserved for action
make in me a new direction.
carry me with the load a my shoulders.
rocks and boulders my friends
the river seems under my feet
walking towards the destiny
My destiny that is meant for me
Crafting my escape, together and bound
way sound the river makes
makes me want to sing and say
father, here is your way.

Paused

The whole world seems in slow motion
continuing the ocean moves me around
aground, run to the sun for shelter
Suddenly everything stops
no running to the shops for drugs & packages
emotion soothed as i no longer need to move
life is paused for a few precious moments
the calm ocean and serenity soothes me.
laying in the late day sun.
breeze brings me comfort and ease
i go to sleep with deep tendencies on my mind
the splash of colour raises my mood
My brew of tea has left me watching
nature and it's calm state
friends come and go, speaking to a sparrow
i stare with comfort and ease
Pause this moment, what to remember
whatever happened to my december?
food chewed, raced my state
Systems broken fear chasing me
to my desk now i am free
i praise my Lord a burden taken
Possibility feels for my safety
because i woke up blessed with a daisy
in the early morning sunshine and dewy grass

Tonight

Where is my light
I sleep safely at night.
Everytime i do wrong it turns into right
Politics as i cast another vote.
I vote for peace
The detached elements recur among us
but not yet at us.
Plus i trust in the right things
I trust in the right people i hope
Slopy moments slippery and wet
dangerous as it seems
Still I land right on my feet
every time
Nothing can break my code
No-one can break my heart anymore
is it strong or is it senseless?
Paving out my heart
as i look the wrong to your ways
chase me down a slippy hill
where the crisp filled hissy eaters are
come to declare spiritual food is better.

63

nest express

To lay a nest in somebody's chest
Suggesting a way to follow my tracks.
no turning back as i lay on it.
brilliance and in all splendour
i chase the stage staggered into a memory
Do you remember when i came here?
Did you see a light oh so clear?
  because i left my past and dwelling
prominently yours even though my mis-spelling
telling me everything i needed to know
around you view you set me to grow
my nest express, a journey so free
Suggesting my term for poverty
honestly i come to you broken
then you made me new and outspoken.
A token of my affection
You erected my stature like a tall home
that you may dwell sincerely alone
Your throne really does reside in me
Validate the ygmred your eastern family
turned away from the adversary
it is all plain to see you growing
lift the lid on the power there is in you
ylaird and faithful, there is always a dove
to draw me close.

64

Today's distress

Calmly choose to bend my friend
send you love but not in ignorance.
Color me in as you take to change
harvesting ways to praise for none
but in truth we are all the same.
Today's distress undressing my nesting layers
laying with changes that spread you ...
it is a blessing you ... to break into song
i could be right or i could be far from wrong.
Songs react to the murmuring yearnings
of my ability to write down that glue
the glue holds my reality together
weathering bold choices and voices
noise prepares me for the day
and then my night.
nightfully i stole the praise you deserve
and i wrote it i can show it
declare what is true, grievances removed
there is no contract ... has my vote
motions you beckon way of life
love are here and i still be you right
some delightly in lifting i work towards peace
hoping my ... carry and dream
such a long time ago
where the tears used to pull loose

Collapsable me

Sensing your indecision
the mission faithfully fought within
Collapsable me, the purest enduring phrase
praise on the lips of the disgusting mind
quickly call me from my own little reality
lightning hot, resisting my calamity
of years and tears ago

fears that can resist progression
mission of working ammunition
release my blood into victorious proposition
truthe that rules the vote of the poor.
down to down i see a sore body
nobody really knows what is underneath
what is there to show beyond what we see?
beneath the riddle is the eye seen.
with one other that pulls my mind
into confusion, useless and broken
but now, a have to bear your chair
Someone elegant, spine ends
i am certain without the choices i made
into your arms i run into your heart
you all there, right from the start
Collapsable me, right you are
call me your and not that too far.
in you with the view of ease.

Moulder

when i came home one day
there was a doctor turning away
down the steps, he went with affray
what a huge at day for ray
portraying his judgment
There was nothing he could do.
crafting irresponsibility, gone
    but Ray feasted
not deterred he went forth
into prayer he leapt into the cold
No soothsayer, no doctor, no nurse
no card readers, money could not do
for they what he really needed
A father whom could change his reality
Sovereign are all
whom else understands or falls
drifting in and out of consciousness
he devises a plan to shed under weight
Rays plate is full and can generate ideals
the mould so the went for those
not willing to dig their toes into me
Plans or hearts that built the city
I cannot and shall not declare bankruptsy
my coffee is full and is no mystery
take me a piece of yr treasury

67

Sports day

The rubble i go through
to make a change in my life.
Sports day has come
Tuned to perfection
Blasting the record, all of them
cheering me and vaccines we made
the trouble with dosage
is that it is illegitimate
mostly you cures are made in sleep
Sleepy desires that tread the yoke
subconsciously i send you up the right one.
Songwriters and singer made
a wonderful beginning staged
the line sends me to another page
if i desire it to do so?
Through the facade i was made a winner
cause ran and finished
no longer a sinner in your eyes
your surprise but knew of my hesitation
reimburse me as you touch the notion.
Your nurture is my main dissertation
Vaccines and my heart is the page
is it true i am meant for the stage?
foraging for a higher purpose
a higher position, i get a little surplus

A platter of the matter

You go round my mind
often go running it around
Sounding out the sorrows of a beggar
and begging for a loan
i shall not beg
the peg that holds me tight
there is hope amongst us
trust in maker to make the right change
Pages you-all for my heavenly wage
ages pass, you remain the same
how long shall i wait
to hear your voice again?
Sanity returns, just.

Adjust my position in this place.
wave me until i see my side change
Charge across the land laid bare
Sobbing and departing
Start my rest and never gauge
you have waited

Painting a Sanity image
can i envisage slimming down
I eat the platter of the matter
it really matters what you take in
take things and make it work
unknown wealth are my forked ways

69

treasure my pet

when i measure what ya leave
it is clear ya are up to take
every mistake we see from ya
give me a chance for relief
constant relief, i need from ya
as ya chew my every member
my membership is always there
it never grows old or easier
Tired of trying to want myself
But as i study
i am in good health
benevolent of all my courage
home to my homeage
wrestling with my vesture
because i find it so difficult
to let go of what i know
ya would call me teachers yet
and ya would ya take it
wrong my? Treasured i am
and i feel the cost ya paid
for me, leave no sound
as i walk, guarding the earth

70

A castaway smile

Every smile you run with
each kiss that satisfies
Don't cast it away
look in dated files
genuinely, i look at you
and i feel tender urging
to guard you from it all.
Cast away the line of duty
because i love you this way.
Paying and praying to you.
You count in a family
to be and talk of destiny.
are you destined to reign?
do you wait the rain?
because it is survival
of the mind that keeps it
intact, but do re-enact
lots of our lives that really
mean something special
to us and others
because those moments
are meant to be enjoyed and
remembered

71

You taught me to live

Surrendering into you via
never resisting my choice
because boys will be boys.
You taught me to live
you taught me to cry.
i find in my eyes.
You are the changer of my heart.
Parting waves but no way
i pray to the most highs for
Plottery same bread crumbs
i love them to be followed.
and when tomorrow comes
in reveils in my head
if you are frozen in time
you cannot stay alive
todays and tomorrows
flowing in patience and relevance
balanced at the top.
the board i cannot leave
until the work is received.
We cannot break the bag
it darkens until we breathe in.

72

Tired of this

Waking up can be a drag
those letters i have seen
Make my wanting jaw sag,
but because it is you
whom drew me so close.
You garders mostly Sew
good seeds and protect them.
Page is my memo
the you is my thoughts
the thoughts are my mind

73

What a carry on

because it is you i feel for
the menace has gone
nothing to be afraid of
carry on regardless
of a forgotten major hassle.
oh, what a carry on
get on with you wheres
you on the greed i have breeded
nothing yet or bleeding
no i have seen you now
because home is your heart
i feel at home with you
fostering and planning
yarning and a future
nurtured into kindness
the harassment decorate
miss-haps happen
but not to us, we trust
safety in you i am blessed
i am the blessed child
ready for nesting
progressing through life.

road crossings.

the wagon tosses to and through
without a care in the world
it is encased in magnificence.
Single eyed it seems
tumbleweed could mark it us
but it doesn't
this pair of horses.
horses that ... the earth
cutting underfoot its brazen way
hay the last thing on its mind
kindly gives without necessity
to bring me home
then i come to a crossing.
the life we live is but a dream.
Seems like you are very near
to me i shuse no fear in us
as we trott and glide a night
flight of a angel.
carries forth the feast
its all or choice
i view my ...
breathing ... to forgiveness

75

Emotion

Ya mostly breeze
down on my knees.
Rattling through the trees.
as the i say:-

It is a joke, this world
i have no idea of this girl
Ascending to me is a far las
something i don't quiet understand

Pearls of wisdom
that bring me comfort
its the system
that brings me pain
Stained quiet washed with blood
making myself understood
and then i call out to you

because i tire easily
presenting a rose to be
punched in adoration.
if you give lady brenda

yess me the communitie
to light my cause
going to the source
Pledging to my committon
that i turned down
because, on the clue
s...

    I sit down and wonder
the battle is won
do i plunder the spoils?
Man(?) yld foiled
Embroiled for this chance
a sentimental sort of elegance
do i buy up this pretense?
and say that, am live
when i am not.

Lulled into comfort
the ball beeps me still
i come to a conclusion
and then i see you face
all conclusion disappears
and then I is you and me
i see colors and a family tree

my heart in truth due
whenever you leave my side
a so i think ....
back for the birds
as i tell my story
i start to sink
into the glory set for me

Pleasantries i am accustomed to
Nurturing fees, it is all here
each is starting to dwell within
and then it leaves
with a goodbye.
My LORD, you know i try
but its not my beggings
and begging is their choice
is it their only choice?

i see a face
and it cannot be erased
leaving this heart of hearts
that quivers in the sea
reaching of possibilities
i sense a freedom

and i am not used to
tolerating foot fall the bruised few
the ones that run away
shouting to ya all
the laws that were set
in no doubt, ya on here send

what is this dark tent?
what is it that made a gent?
but are i gain
i am a conscious arse again
of the food that feeds my brain
it is another cold day
its the way i declair ya now
it's so all about you
that makes me stay sane
brotherly love
and a smashed glass window
from the fragility of your name
i sense ya near
right beside to my face

Entangled but rested
and now i am ousted

Passing at

because of my curiosity
i pity the man
who slips through viscosity
Sympathetic to the ear
Steering the courage
and coming in with the tide
as i miss-lives y re kil.
it cracked and exploded
Passing of in stock
tumbling and wrestling
night trance testing
y stop as you near to go on
tender mercies
come y dragging my side
her side, sliding down
sliding beneath
i hold back my heart.
wanting a few to come b.
up day the hill
us my name a high
Surprise the few,
And lead my sky

triumphant and majestic
i try to ride well
dying inside the well.
empty but plenty.
all stories told, thoughts
its ages.
better you did empty
than full of empty promises
honestly, sense you worth
you wait and weight
you really are.
when, sense you laying
i shall take you
sensing a finished purpose
time to reap the rewards
surplus to expectations
p never made sure
it has love doll things give
living in victory
is not from and far
I bring you closer
and always have won
escaping you future,
is my wish in you complete.

i enjoy what a date
my friend was closer
is it time for my yay?
drawing you closer
i aim to please.
my memories come back
to life within me
chasing them into the distance
a slight remembrance
occurs sometimes
but buried beneath
the overturn hill
resting my body
unlisted her misery
histories of good appraised.
found my color
inside an abrasive material
passing all for good
i muscle in on thy will
veins and every color
seems to me like in another
passed down through the years
colors in the mind
not yesterdays of so now.

a wondrous thud

because you are whom you are
people will stop and stare
sometimes right through you
your world shelves speak of love.
Then, i heard you
he paid the full cost
  because i am who i am
Standing a holy, solid ground
surrounded in peace and harmony
sylish you i am there
Pools of your water soothe me
yesterday i chose to see
full and elegant
  Full of love and memmorial
pass me the life given
bread and wine, as Jesus
speaking thanking us, he us
where we clarify the scene
been once to a distinct group
no more i say
in and with me LORD,
his tube feeds me

The Ship

Scorn due to past mistakes
i see my food that was eaten
on the floor i find myself
the ship tugged me away
dis-used in an elementary way
substituted because i was weak
to weak to fight by myself
the cold mind black
Sails on side for scream,
give me your may.
i can make good use how it
is the mornings i wake up,
with little notices of regret
oject from the headache
of my yapping regrets
that kept me banded.
repeating mistakes again
time well felt
I know the height you felt
was just about consolable
resting next for the table
where drink and food
enable conversation

84

living my dreams.

Sending my thoughts airward
into the sky of a lived sunrise
realsing you are under me too.
letting me into recognition
missionaries heartfelt wishes.
funches comes for and have me
and i scan the land
as it lays wastey
but be careful of people
they want many and diverse
my hardly youic
when i display characteristic
if a man gone mad
but not quietu i say
may i say a single thought?
drawn in from my youth.
roses and Photograph.
they can want you know
but don't cast me aside
because it hurts
graphically i can make
my dreams come true.

I beg me

looking in the forgotten mirror
i forget what i look like
but it tries i remember
there are looking back at me.
i am handsome a reasoned
because i know it is still there
my watch tells me my time
My time is now
coming back into vision
into sight i thought the heights
of dizzy cumbersome delights
I beg myself not to look.
it disturbs me
not knowing who i am
planning my daydreams
my father dresses me perfect
seems to me like i had a proposal
rushing by my adventures
gradually i come to believe
that i obey the real
bruised by it
because if i'm not bruised, it
didn't hurt a head

classes are see-through.

Masses turn to yr hopes
remote and far away
classes rasp each other
the delights and other insight
tearing at the seams.
the light is red and my dear
run for cover, protected
ive been running for too long.
now it calls for my action
this memory of a silent mode.
today is the memory
that kept me pure and happy.
was i only an empty shell?
my bell has stopped working
i am undeserving of these
treasures kept for me.
i doubt if they are waiting
devastating for me and you.
if i stay for a show of my life
would i cringe?
would i be ashamed?
i am reassured i shall not

Victory

I shamed my own defensia
detained from humanity
lost years elementary dear friends
but in the end
it means little to know why
trying to know how it came to be
wish my benevolence and duty
and go out into the world
where rats where scalves
and the demise is a unwise choice
it is a long long way it seems.
buffering the heads of noise
it is only noise
but it is all we have
i take at the bag
my choice as i go dancing
Auroboros, the victory song
 places me up into order
giving me a reason to be
searching the sea for treasure
measuring my chances
a return to my life

Talk

You hold it all away from me
but your thoughts are like the sea.
shimmering in the sunshine.
glistening in the wake
because it is so near that time
to say goodbye to belongings
talking of natural days
sensing half of my refunded pay
settle me as i go away
and bear the man behind
the purse i was nor the soul i am
commend my effords
for with such hope i was born
i delight in your conversation
run me away, the blood has paid
my debts and debtors
blood dissolving into the distance
parades would not be enough
i sense your courageous heart
loved ones shall pay their respects
doubled for the journey
young, but full of life

Despair

i caught the train
to a foreign place.
mainly because i knew
that if i didn't i would have no chance
review my thoughts and hope
of walking and playing
portraying the wilderness
And i thought i was in
twinned with a bunch
a taboo as hunch
That really broke me.
i say that in a senseless state
it is all separated
this life is no longer mine
forced into a corner.
bordering on an elastic waistline
Time is a strange thing
we think we have it
but it is just drifting away
as you play with your guns
people are dying every minute
i live there scarless in their
state of being

Pulse

Pulsating with empty lives
they grab with little retrieve
emotions that are hidden
come out of their domain
slowly cut into pieces
realise i release their hurts
flirting with insanity
lying in the state of anxiety
quietly she goes home
and then relieves her pulse
just for a few minuets
while she takes a visit
to some meds, just the end
they are everywhere
i cannot hide the fact now
perhaps it is about me
living in the state, waiting for death
but life comes and topples it
comes in with authority
washing away addled effects
to renew you of gravity
but that is not the truth

91

Correct Attire

Standing back as i admire you
the mirror cannot hold you
because all you say is true
news of the missing traffickers,
deploying and exploiting possibilities
chasing the momentary bliss
i dug out due to foreign aid
paid expenses, voted leases
suggest i am already here
chained you like the wind
winding up my adversaries
not care to steal and destroy
plays to discard my body
a cocoon waiting
for a concerned love
to give meat to the bones
i grow to see you never
because i care for you
and all of you exhibits
brand new, all of you
dressed to express
you took the park

heading for a mind

In its entirety i succumb
to a yawning illusion
where we are better in hope
if the greatest figures
My world and niche shelter you
and make you real
feel you way through life
i must have lost scope
and i have to cope with miss-direction
A new location a dis-location
from those pressing issues
used to be for love and hope
but now all i see
is gatings and dope
rummaging through town.
bins, the floor, the beds
he knows there is little time
everything that i declare
comes straight from the heart
together we are laiden, but
i am heading for the mind
to cure and protect you

93

live under your

the hot tar heals like a oven
as spread like endless feet
correcting the curves and bumps
hiding what is left, adding
a circumference of lain bodies
you feel live under your
but the tar is seeping
it's way through the steel
soon you could be hidden
but you won't be
because i can your voice
i choose you as a friend
no matter for the carriage
or you are ushered into safety
live under your.
you could be walking oh so far
jars of dreams kept on the shelf
jarring the news as a presence
Surely LORD you will forget
my passing ones.
During my time, singled out
for glory

Naturally yours

I follow the trail
of my lost bitter mail
the mail came home
to the rescue i own it
plans we have to sort pity
put it in it's box
a weighty reminder
of who i am destined to be
seeing you grow in stature
makes my heart tick
in a natural remedy
my father lives inside of me
naturally yours to hold
growing in spirit
as i kick dust off my feet
but i tend to be forward
sticking in the air
passing through
until i meet the shore
i saw you and your growth
you shall stand
and never be alone.

The key is hidden

...push to open the door
...all of you might
stressed and torn
not a hair to God
being reborn is not a plight
...ideal
hiding the key to your future
it could be right under your nose
...and lillies
...but beauty
...soon ...
into the distance of correction
correction towards the start
...heart, ...
...familiarity of praise
the maze is broken,
...key ... ...all to see
...Jesus, you are the
...my battles
...turmoil and struggle
...desire, and never
...exhume

Set to Serve

My Jesus, my Star
the brighter you shine
the more i yearn for you
Please don't stay on far
you came to serve.
how lovely.
breathing life into us
the whole planet.
When you were needed
You are there, close to touch
You are much and deservedly
the one we praise and say thanks
[?] you fields of humility
Setting captives free
i was down, now i am able
to walk this walk
and to set your table, one day
I say to others your kindness.
and towards me a Softness
And grace and strength so
like a pillow for a restful sleep
You declare your portion, are you
will be.

Shock.

all the courage i amassed
wont take payment
the gentle vibration
of my loves heart
but some time it races
it takes me to the finish line
then it is all up to me
shock comes when least expected
neglecting to tell me your
life in the back has you
instead yours is all that's left
it reigns, plainly speaking
i have enough of the plan
even if i find a new day
do i want new days?
shock until ready for change
with her looking into the distance
what am i letting out
over the years i've gained?
gaining a steady useless beat
this is why i eat the word
taking back what is mine.

touch

when i think of you love
i feel it deep inside
when i feel you touch
ya humming my keys
touching my mind at best
really gives me a thrill.
running my the steady mill
until you are absorbed into me
you make me breathe easy
ya see the good in me
Such touching moments
really does raise the rod
the floor is no-longer hard
kould be worried for everyone
but my father makes a way
you evangelical alliance
brightening day
come will to me
it really does matter
because the gate is always open
A token of my love at you can
come to me with all your burden

99

Down amongst the grass

capitalist movement
Shiver in my mind,
When first gone bad
i design my way to release
myself from the pressures
of everyday necessities
better yet to bail out in tears
than to sit emotionless
I wish you knew you can feel.
i sit here surrounded by items
emotionless, uncaring, lifeless items
Then there is you
Full of beauty and wisdom
long suffering gainful picture
falling in the joys it gives
when no-one else would
nothing a backlash of fraud run
i have much to say of you
hidden in the grass
we will make this last
things pass as we know
under/an wonderful shame and tell.

Interviewing

The last of harmony.

Trying to buy someone else's life
euthanasia, protection, regeneration
blinds the thoughts of a protagonist.
most would sense a relief
but i am solemn
choosing to write and create.
a special friend, a good mate
Collapse into a wordy of hope
colours cascading into one
one bright light needed many colours
the last of harmony.
take it out try and fix it.
Silence beggars and vagabonds
we can eat all of these things
bring me my sense of hope
bring me my senses not cage
and write my story with me
leading me hastily on silent ground
firm in a state of shock
running me around the clock
packed into one little box
hopes for all including the little fox

To my friend connected

home alone is where i am from
carving my way through life
this problem weighs a ton
then i start tripping occasionally
it all comes down to common sense
sometimes i have it
sometimes i don't
cant wait shall and will not
its all excuses as i say
i must calm my mind
because with you
i have owned and twisted the road
connected, even though i dont see you
we have the strength
i know you will pull me through
entertainment in the mind
the way i fought
hardest to me blind
Signed and dated
found my luck manna tasted
I will not be down to her
not this time.

uncommon sense

lets not pretend it is not there
shading thee sad and alone
my tone needs tweaking
& i bear the stare unturned
do you have sympno a uncommon sense?
for me i don if i dare to.
what are you gonna come to?
blue and then away
on the scrap heap.
i still not and will not
take responsibility for it.
i sit, i wonder, i ponder
the best course of action
then an chanced inaction
re-acting to the yarn
drizzled and fizzled and
clouding my mind and visia
was she to veal?
was it her ammunition?
that sent me spiralling?
no-one can take away
my schooling and claim my
reward

True

Is it true not you false?
Is it true you telling?
Where are you heading
Me as not don't pretend.
Me falsehood is
that you really defend your choices
voices your voice

Is it true
not there can feed you
For because they die
Surprisingly you came here alone
Morning you our taste
is taste you nod your choices
take a little time away to think
take a while
You are a the proud of greatness
create in me voice
eh was not breathe into you
they follow you yeah
in your eyes
help turning the pages
truthfully yours

Printed in the United States
by Baker & Taylor Publisher Services